T0198799

HERO AT HOME

by Sarah Verardo

Illustrated by Inna Eckman
Photography by Lindsay Hart

HERO AT HOME

iUniverse books may be ordered through booksellers or by contacting:

iUniverse
1663 Liberty Drive
Bloomington, IN 47403
www.iuniverse.com
1-800-Authors (1-800-288-4677)

ISBN: 978-1-5320-5954-4 (sc)
ISBN: 978-1-5320-5955-1 (e)
ISBN: 978-1-5320-5953-7 (hc)

Library of Congress Control Number: 2018911855

Print information available on the last page.

iUniverse rev. date: 11/19/2020

Dedication

To the men of Bravo Company, 2-508th Parachute
Infantry Regiment, 82nd Airborne.

For the ones who gave their lives, the ones who saved
Mike, and the ones who live with the aftermath of it all.

You and your families have my heart.

Foreword by
U.S. Senator Elizabeth Dole

Early in our relationship, my husband, Senator Bob Dole, asked to explain his combat wounds to my mother. Bob said, "Mrs. Hanford, I think you ought to see my problem." Looking at his scars, my mother replied, "Bob, that's not a problem. That's a badge of honor."

In HERO AT HOME, Sarah Verardo teaches Americans of every age how to view the wounds of our veterans with that same level of understanding and compassion. Through a sweet and patriotic tale, Sarah reminds our nation of the pride and respect we owe those who served and their loved ones.

HERO AT HOME comes at a time when our nation needs it most. The Elizabeth Dole Foundation has found that the millions of children growing up in wounded veteran families feel both the pride of their families' service and the tremendous stress of their ongoing struggles. America has yet to realize the full impact of this experience, yet we know for sure that our wounded veterans' children require every bit of patience, understanding, and support our nation can offer them.

As a devoted wife and caregiver to Mike, doting mother to three beautiful young girls, and committed veteran and caregiver advocate, there is no one more qualified than Sarah to write this story. I encourage every family and classroom in America to read HERO AT HOME and discuss the timeless American values it teaches us.

This is Grace's Dad.

He wanted to serve in the United States Army as an infantryman with the 82nd Airborne to protect the freedom of all Americans.

He was sent to Afghanistan to protect
America, and was Wounded in Action
while fighting for our country.

He wears a special leg that looks
like it belongs on a robot.

His arm was rebuilt with lots of tools.

Sometimes he uses a wheelchair.

His outdoor wheelchair goes very fast
and can go in sand, snow, and the woods.

Grace and her little sisters take
turns riding in his lap.

Grace's Dad is still working
hard to get better.

He rests and goes to the doctor a lot.

Every morning Grace helps her Daddy's
nurse check his heart, head, and lungs.

Sometimes he is sad because he
misses his friends who didn't
come home to their families.

Noises, smells, and experiences can
remind him of being back in war.

Grace's Dad has a brain injury.

Sometimes he makes mistakes
like putting keys in the fridge
and milk in the closet.

Grace, her sisters, and their
Mom help him with his day.

Grace's Dad tells her that sometimes people get hurt and their bodies change, but they still have the same heart.

Grace's Dad has lots of friends that
also have new arms and legs.

They are all American heroes!

THE END

ABOUT THE AUTHOR

SARAH VERARDO

Sarah Verardo is a national advocate for wounded Veterans and their Caregivers. Her husband Michael was catastrophically wounded in Afghanistan in 2010, in two separate IED attacks that took his left leg, much of his left arm, and left him with polytraumatic conditions that have required more than one hundred surgeries and years of speech, visual, physical and occupational therapies. Starting as a volunteer with The Independence Fund, Sarah's steadfast devotion, experience, and drive led to her eventual selection as the organization's first Chief Executive Officer. Sarah carries on the legacy of The Independence Fund's founder by continuing the hallmark all-terrain track wheelchair program to provide mobility to wounded heroes.

Sarah advises Administration officials and members of Congress on the experiences of the families of our severely wounded Veterans and has been instrumental in shaping national policy for our warfighters and their families. Regularly appearing on cable news to commentate on the sacrifice of Veterans and Military families, Sarah is a respected subject matter expert in the field.

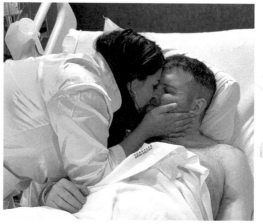

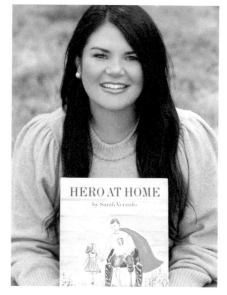

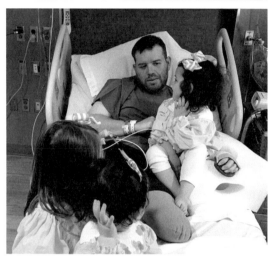

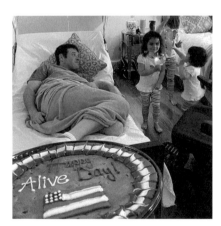

ABOUT THE INDEPENDENCE FUND

Founded in 2007, The Independence Fund is committed to empowering our nation's catastrophically wounded, injured, or ill Veterans to overcome physical, mental, and emotional wounds incurred in the line of duty. We are dedicated to improving the lives of both our Veterans and their families.

Through our programs, we support the Veterans who have come home wounded, injured or ill and those standing by their side.

We give INDEPENDENCE back to these heroes.

And so can YOU...

CREATE AN IMPACT

Donate. Volunteer. Support.
To learn more about The Independence Fund or ways to get involved, please visit **www.independencefund.org**

THE
INDEPENDENCE
— FUND —

100% of the proceeds from the sales of "Hero at Home" will directly support the mission of The Indepdence Fund.

Printed in the United States
by Baker & Taylor Publisher Services